ARIZONA TREES: AN INTRODUCTION

This 'Easy Field Guide' is one of a series of similar books covering the more interesting plants and animals of Arizona. We have found that many guides are too complicated for the layman. We have selected 47 of the most common species of trees to include in this guide. Rare and very local species have been omitted. Included are those characters and facts which we feel you will find particularly useful in identifying the tree in question. Keep in mind that all leaves, even those from the same tree, may show some variation.

Since elevations in Arizona range from about sea-level in the southwestern deserts to over 12,000 feet at the highest point, there are a great many different habitats for trees. This is reflected in a great variety of trees, from the Ironwood which grows only in frost-free areas to old Bristlecone Pines that grow near timberline. We think that you will find this guide very useful and enjoy discovering (for yourself) many new kinds of trees.

MEXICAN PINYON:
1 1/2-inch needles in groups of 3; typical 'pinyon' cone about 1 inch high; small tree common in s.e. Arizona mountains; 5,000-7,000 ft.

COLORADO PINYON:
1 1/2-inch needles in groups of 2; typical 'pinyon' cone; common in n. Arizona; 5,000-7,000 ft.

SINGLELEAF PINYON:
1 1/2-inch needles in 'groups' of 1; cone larger than those of the other pinyons; similar to Colorado Pinyon; scattered localities in nothern Arizona; 4,000-6,000 ft.

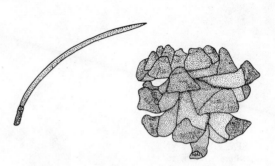

BRISTLECONE PINE:
3/4-inch needles in groups of 5; found only in San Francisco Peaks from about 9,000 ft. to timberline; purplish cones about 3 inches long; small, sharp structures on cones

LIMBER PINE:
2 1/2-inch needles in groups of 5; very large cones (about 6 inches long); no sharp points on cones; common in mountains; 6,000-10,000 ft.

CHIHUAHUA PINE:

3- to 4-inch needles in groups of 3; somewhat resembles longer-needled Ponderosa Pine; needle groups which have fallen to the ground have lost their sheaths while those of Ponderosa Pine haven't; needles of Chihuahua Pine are thinner than those of Ponderosa Pine; cones have definite stalks and remain on the tree for long periods; s.e. Arizona mountains; 5,000-7,000 ft.

PONDEROSA PINE:
Needles in groups of 3 (sometimes 5); needles 5-7 inches long; abundant, often very large tree; often occurs in huge stands; bark often reddish brown with puzzle-like appearance of flaking bark when viewed closely; compare with less common Chihuahua and Apache Pines; 5,000-7,500 ft.

APACHE PINE:

Very long needles (10 inches or more) in groups of 3; needles often 1/16 inch wide or more, those of Ponderosa Pine thinner; tree often appears similar to Ponderosa Pine, but in addition to above differences, the sheaths around the needles of Apache Pine are often 3/4-inch or longer, those of Ponderosa Pine are less; mountains and canyons of s.e. Arizona; 5,000-7,000 ft.

ENGELMANN SPRUCE:

Needles not in groups; needles 4-sided, about 3/4-inch long with a sharp tip; small twigs have bumps on them where needles were attached; 2-inch-long cones have thin scales; high mountains; 8,500 ft. to timberline

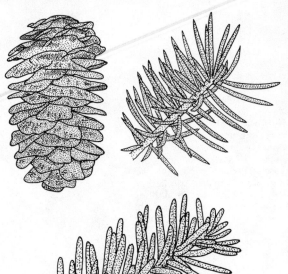

ALPINE FIR:

Needles not in groups; needles 1 1/2 inches long, tending to be fatter toward their bases; upright, purplish cones on the tree are easiest means of identification; cones 3 inches long, but fall apart while still on the tree; a high mountain tree; 8,000 ft. to timberline

DOUGLAS FIR:

Needles not in groups; needles 1 inch long, flattened and with a thin indentation running the length on top; cones distinctive, with 3-pointed structured sticking out between scales; cones about 2 inches long; common in cooler areas of mountains; 6,000-10,000 ft.

WHITE FIR:

Needles not in groups; needles flattened and from 1-3 inches long; where needles attach to twigs they have a sucker-like appearance; needles lack indentation along top; cones fall to pieces when mature and lack 3-pointed structures of Douglas Fir; often small tree; cool mountain areas; 6,000-9,000 ft.

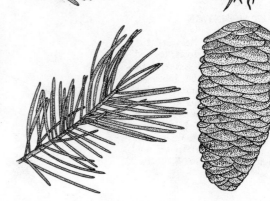

ALLIGATOR JUNIPER:

Small, scale-like leaves; bark distinctive, being divided into "squares" resembling back of an alligator; berry about 1/2-inch in diameter and grayish-green; common in mountains; 4,000-7,000 ft.

ROCKY MOUNTAIN JUNIPER:

Small, scale-like leaves; has many similarities to One-Seed and Utah Junipers but can be distinguished by the following combination of characters: Usually a single main trunk; 1/4-inch, bluish berry, usually with 2 seeds, and juicy when squeezed; tips of small branchlets (and leaves) flattened and hanging down; 5,500-8,500 ft.

ONE-SEED JUNIPER:

Small, scale-like leaves; distinguished from Rocky Mountain and Utah Junipers by the following combination of characters: Usually smaller tree with many small trunks coming out from below or near ground level; lacks a single main trunk; berries 1/4-inch in diameter and purplish-blue, usually juicy and with only 1 seed; trees of 2 separate sexes, berries on the females, pollen on the males

UTAH JUNIPER:

Small, scale-like leaves; distinguished from Rocky Mountain and One-Seed Junipers by the following combination of characters: Has a single main trunk with branches coming off lower down than in the case of the Rocky Mountain Juniper; berries fibrous inside rather than juicy as in the other two species; 3,500-7,000 ft.

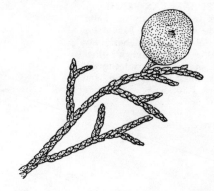

ARIZONA CYPRESS:
Small, scale-like leaves; cones more-or-less round and about 3/4 inch in diameter; cones divided into sections, each with a small mound on it; bark grayish with vertical 'scars;' along creeks in mountain canyons; sometimes large tree; 4,000-7,000 ft.

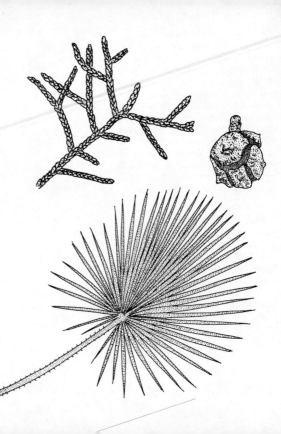

CALIFORNIA FAN PALM:
Grows in wild, only in Palm Canyon in the Kofa Mountains south of Quartzite; our only species of native palm; all other palms in cities are introduced; leaves about 5 feet long, fan shaped; 2,500 ft.

NARROWLEAF COTTONWOOD:

Leaves spear shaped; leaf length 3-4 inches, usually less than 1 inch wide; leaf edges with fine teeth; often large tree; along creeks; 5,000-6,500 ft.

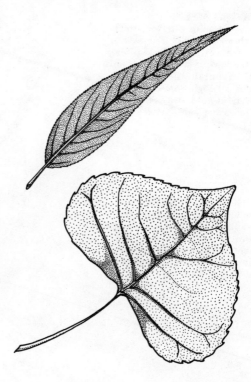

FREMONT COTTONWOOD:

Triangular-shaped leaves with long, flattened (side to side) stems; leaf edges with uneven teeth; very common, large tree along streams at lower elevations; near sea-level to 5,000 ft.

QUAKING ASPEN:
Leaves roundish with long stems which are flattened from side to side where they join the leaf blade; bark whitish; grows on cool mountain slopes; leaves flutter in slight breezes; forms beautiful gold and yellow autumn colors; 7,000-9,500 ft.

GOODDING WILLOW:
The largest of the many species of willows found in Arizona; narrow leaves 3-5 inches long, about 1/2 inch wide; sometimes a large tree; along streams; near sea-level to 6,000 ft.

ARIZONA WALNUT:
Entire leaf about 12 inches long with 10 or more leaflets coming off main stem; each leaflet about 3 inches long, 1 inch wide; look for walnuts on ground; these have a fibrous outer husk and a hard inner shell; common along streams and washes; 4,000-6,000 ft.

ARIZONA ALDER:
Leaves about 3 inches long; edges with small teeth; small 'cones' about 1/2 inch long; common along edges of creeks; 5,000-6,000 ft.

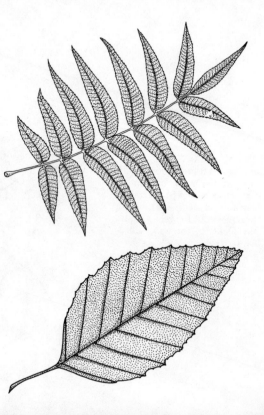

NETLEAF OAK:
Leaves about 3 inches long, very thick and leathery; bottom of leaf concave with distinct raised veins; top of leaf dark green (compare with lighter Arizona White Oak); in canyons; 4,000-6,000 ft.

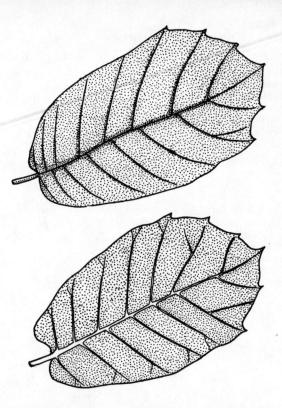

ARIZONA WHITE OAK:
Leaves similar to those of Netleaf Oak, but Arizona White Oak leaves are usually more than twice as long as wide--those of Netleaf less; leaf often thick and somewhat leathery as with Netleaf; top of leaf light green; 5,000-7,000 ft.

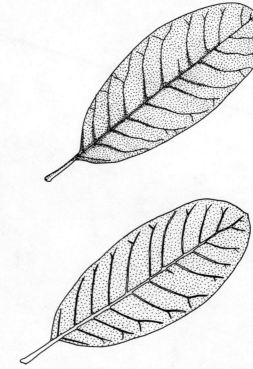

MEXICAN BLUE OAK:
Leaves with distinctive oblong shape, about 1 1/2 inches long; no teeth on leaf edges; ends of leaves rounded and base indented; tops of leaves often a bluish-green color; southern Arizona mountains; 5,000-6,000 ft.

GRAY OAK:
Leaves about 1 to 1 1/2 inches long, pointed at tip; leaf tends to be somewhat heart-shaped; leaf edge usually without teeth; top of leaf shiny, bottom somewhat hairy; 5,000-6,000 ft.

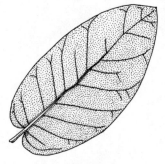

GAMBEL OAK:
Leaves with distinctive lobes; leaves about 3-6 inches long; unlike our other oaks, loses leaves in winter; common small tree on cool mountain slopes; 5,000-7,500 ft.

EMORY OAK:
Leaves 1 to 2 1/2 inches long; edges often with a few sharp teeth or edges smooth (both leaf types often on same tree); both top and bottom of leaf shiny; two fuzzy spots at base of leaf on bottom; very common in southern Arizona mountains; 4,000-6,500 ft.

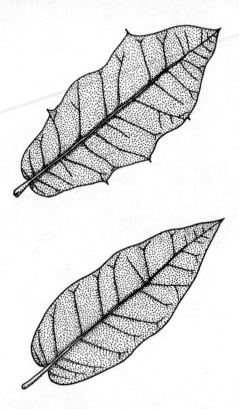

SILVERLEAF OAK:
Leaves spear shaped, pointed at tip; leaves 3-4 inches long, about 3/4 inch wide; tops of leaves green, bottoms a fuzzy white ("silver"); edges of leaves curl under; common in mountains; 5,500-7,500 ft.

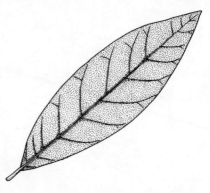

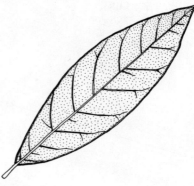

NETLEAF HACKBERRY:
Leaves with "off-center," somewhat heart-shaped appearance; leaves 1-3 inches long, usually with 3 main veins coming from stem; top of leaf coarse to touch, bottom with raised veins; along washes; small tree; 2,000-5,500 ft.

COMMON CHOKECHERRY:
Leaf about 3 inches long; top darker than bottom; leaf edges with teeth; small tree along streams in mountains; reddish fruit with large seed; 5,000-7,500 ft.

ARIZONA SYCAMORE:
Leaves large (5-9 inches long and wide) with star-like shape; common tree along creeks; bark whitish; picturesque, spreading branches; ball-shaped fruits have long stems and are often found dried on ground; 2,500-6,500 ft.

HONEY MESQUITE:

Leaves with 9 or more pairs of small leaflets; twigs with stout, paired, yellowish spines; note shape of 4-7 inch pod; abundant along desert washes and grasslands; compare with ScrewBean Mesquite and Ironwood; sea-level to 4,000 ft.

SCREWBEAN MESQUITE:

Leaves with 8 or fewer pairs of small leaflets; twigs with thin, white, paired spines; pods spiral-shaped and about 1-2 inches long; compare with Honey Mesquite and Ironwood; sea-level to 4,000 ft.

FOOTHILL PALOVERDE:

Young stems and parts of bark yellow-green; leaflets, when present, usually 4 or more pairs on each tiny stem; leaflets less than 1/8 inch long; pods constricted between seeds and with point at tip; common in deserts; 1,000-3,500 ft.

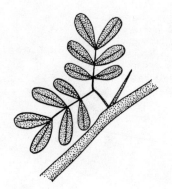

BLUE PALOVERDE:

Young stems with bluish-green bark; leaflets, when present, usually longer than 1/8 inch, and usually 3 or fewer pairs of leaflets on each tiny stem; pod not greatly constricted but somewhat flattened; desert washes; sea-level to 3,500 ft.

IRONWOOD:

Leaves with paired, gray-colored leaflets; individual leaflets 1/2-3/4 inch long; compare with green-barked paloverdes and the two mesquites; usually keeps leaves throughout the year, other similar appearing trees don't; pods hairy with only a few constrictions; along washes; 500-2,500 ft.

NEW MEXICAN LOCUST:

Large shrub or small tree; leaves 8-12 inches long, each leaf with 13 or more leaflets; individual leaflets 3/4 to 1 1/2 inches long and with small point at end; stems with paired spines; flat pods 3-4 inches long; mountains; 5,000-8,000 ft.

NARROWLEAF HOPTREE:
Leaves with 3 leaflets; leaflets 1 to 2 1/2 inches long; surface of leaflets with tiny glands which emit a strong odor; seed with flattened, rounded wing and small stalk; seed plus wings about 1/2 inch across; small tree in mountain canyons; 4,000-8,000 ft.

INLAND BOXELDER:
Leaves with 3 or 5 leaflets, the middle leaflets on a stalk; leaflets 3-4 inches long and edges with large teeth; seeds in pairs with wings; along creeks in canyons and mountains; 4,000-7,000 ft.

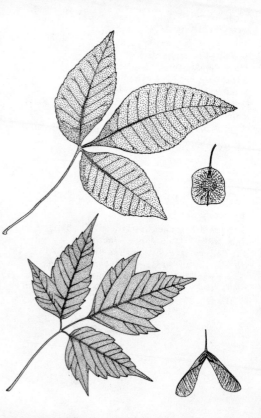

ROCKY MOUNTAIN MAPLE:
Two types of leaves may be present--one not divided, the other divided into 3 leaflets-leaf edges with big teeth which have smaller teeth on them; leaves turn red in autumn; seeds in pairs with wings; along creeks in pine forests; 7,500-9,000 ft.

BIGTOOTH MAPLE:
Leaves 3-5 inches long; each leaf with 3 main lobes; points on leaves are blunt; leaves thicker than those of Rocky Mountain Maple; seeds in pairs with wings; pine forests; 5,000-7,500 ft.

ARIZONA MADRONE:
Leaves spear shaped, 1 to 2 1/2 inches long; distinctive bark a reddish color and very thin, usually peeling in many spots; leaves rather thick, some with smooth edges, others with small teeth; scattered locales in s. Arizona mountains; 4,500-7,500 ft.

VELVET ASH:
Leaf divided into 5-8 leaflets, each leaflet 1 to 2 1/2 inches long; distinctive seed has a long wing on it; seed plus wing about 1 inch long, with wing usually not longer than seed; seeds are not paired and occur in groups; along creeks; 2,500-6,500 ft.

DESERT-WILLOW:
Distinctive leaves very long in relation to width; often 5 or more inches long and less than 1/2 inch wide; seed pods very long, often as long as or longer than leaves and as little as 1/4 inch in diameter; pods stay on all winter; desert washes; 2,000-4,500 ft.

CHECKLIST AND SCIENTIFIC NAMES

- [ ] Mexican Pinyon-*Pinus cembroides*
- [ ] Colorado Pinyon-*Pinus edulis*
- [ ] Singleleaf Pinyon-*Pinus monophylla*
- [ ] Bristlecone Pine-*Pinus aristata*
- [ ] Limber Pine-*Pinus flexilis*
- [ ] Chihuahua Pine-*Pinus chihuahuana*
- [ ] Ponderosa Pine-*Pinus ponderosa*
- [ ] Apache Pine-*Pinus latifolia*
- [ ] Engelmann Spruce-*Picea engelmanni*
- [ ] Alpine Fir-*Abies lasiocarpa*
- [ ] Douglas Fir-*Pseudotsuga taxifolia*
- [ ] White Fir-*Abies concolor*
- [ ] Alligator Juniper-*Juniperus deppeana*
- [ ] Rocky Mountain Juniper-*Juniperus scopulorum*
- [ ] One-Seed Juniper-*Juniperus monosperma*
- [ ] Utah Juniper-*Juniperus osteosperma*
- [ ] Arizona Cypress-*Cupressus arizonica*
- [ ] California Fan Palm-*Washingtonia filifera*
- [ ] Quaking Aspen-*Populus tremuloides*
- [ ] Narrowleaf Cottonwood-*Populus angustifolia*
- [ ] Fremont Cottonwood-*Populus fremontii*
- [ ] Goodding Willow-*Salix gooddingii*
- [ ] Arizona Walnut-*Juglans major*
- [ ] Arizona Alder-*Alnus oblongifolia*

CHECKLIST AND SCIENTIFIC NAMES

- ☐ **Netleaf Oak**-*Quercus reticulata*
- ☐ **Arizona White Oak**-*Quercus arizonica*
- ☐ **Mexican Blue Oak**-*Quercus oblongifolia*
- ☐ **Gray Oak**-*Quercus grisea*
- ☐ **Gambel Oak**-*Quercus gambelii*
- ☐ **Emory Oak**-*Quercus emoryi*
- ☐ **Silverleaf Oak**-*Quercus hypoleucoides*
- ☐ **Netleaf Hackberry**-*Celtis reticulata*
- ☐ **Common Chokecherry**-*Prunus virginiana*
- ☐ **Arizona Sycamore**-*Platanus wrightii*
- ☐ **Honey Mesquite**-*Prosopis juliflora*
- ☐ **Screwbean Mesquite**-*Prosopis pubescens*
- ☐ **Foothill Paloverde**-*Cercidium microphyllum*
- ☐ **Blue Paloverde**-*Cercidium floridum*
- ☐ **Ironwood**-*Olneya tesota*
- ☐ **New Mexican Locust**-*Robinia neomexicana*
- ☐ **Narrowleaf Hoptree**-*Ptelea angustifolia*
- ☐ **Inland Boxelder**-*Acer negundo*
- ☐ **Rocky Mountain Maple**-*Acer glabrum*
- ☐ **Bigtooth Maple**-*Acer grandidentatum*
- ☐ **Arizona Madrone**-*Arbutus arizonica*
- ☐ **Velvet Ash**-*Fraxinus velutina*
- ☐ **Desert Willow**-*Chilopsis linearis*